drowning in reverse

Malia K. Auri

CHAPTERS

Chapter One

Drowning

the weight of the world
holds me down
like ocean waves
and i feel powerless
to fight back

-drowning

i fear
that our generation
spends so much time
looking down at phones
that we might be
forgetting
to look up
at the stars

-look up at the stars

you will never be
too much
or
not enough
for the right person

*-don't settle for someone who can't love you for
who you are*

the moment my lips
touched your lips
i swear if felt
i n f i n i t e

-infinite

never settle for someone
who doesn't give you
consistency

if they're not sure
you're meant to be together
you aren't

-consistency

there is nothing quite as comforting
as curling up in bed
with a good book
listening to the rain
and getting lost
in other worlds

-in love with reading

love someone today
more than they deserve

you never know
when some small act
could change
someone's whole world

-small acts of kindness make the world spin

life may be hard right now
but you
are the caterpillar
about to blossom
into a butterfly

keep your head up
things will get better
i promise

-butterfly in waiting

blessed are those
who remain kindhearted
even when the world
never shows them
that same kindness
in return

-blessed are the kindhearted

in the darkest of times
you find out
who is really
by your side

cherish those people
with everything you have

-cherish

we are all human
we all make mistakes

forgive when you can
for it frees the soul

-forgiveness frees the soul

there is nothing like the excitement
of sending a risky text
and seeing them reply
as possibilities
unfold

-possibilities

never let a man
pressure you
into doing things
you aren't comfortable with

if he can't respect your body
he'll never love your mind

-demand respect

people change
that's a fact of life

sometimes we have to accept
that the person we once loved
no longer exists
though their heart beats on
and their lungs draw breath

-accepting change

he caught my teardrop
with his finger
and wiped it away
promising
everything
would be
alright

-promises

you can't expect
the fire that burned you
to heal you

don't go back to people
who hurt you
expecting to find
healing

-healing

if aliens could see
what we've done to our planet
i doubt they would even want
to meet us

we are monsters
when left to our worst instincts
destroying our world
for a few extra dollars

-monsters

he may have left you
feeling like you're
bleeding

but that's nothing
you haven't been through
before

your ability to
hold yourself together
is stronger than his ability
to break you

-you are stronger

blank canvas
the most
daunting task

it strikes fear
into even the best
of artists

-blank canvas

it's okay to make mistakes
as long
as you learn from them

we are all just learning as we go
no one has it figured out

so don't stress
over your past.

-it's okay to make mistakes

surround yourself
with people
you want to be
more like.

-the right people

always remember
that there is a difference
between being patient with someone
and just wasting your time

-some people just need to be left behind

know what you want in life
and don't stop trying
until you get it

-life

take encouragement
when people talk down on your name

it just means they know
you're headed for greatness
and they don't want
to see you get there

-don't be discouraged

i want to wake up next to you
every morning

i want to spoil you
with breakfast in bed

i want to love you
till the day i die

-forever love

Chapter Two

Falling

i fell for you hard
and there's no getting up

-yours

i look at your face
and pray to god
that i never
have to lose you

-dear god

don't be afraid
to take time for yourself
when you need it

-self-care

you
were the sunlight
and i
was the flower

-your flower

there's nothing wrong
with being wrong

just accept it
and learn
from your mistakes

-flourish

you have to fall in love
with yourself
before you can love
someone else

-steps

when your vision
seems cloudy
search within
and trust your gut

it always knows
the right choice
before you do

-trust your instincts

it hurts
to not be with you

this
is how much
i love you

-addict

commitment
is the glue
that keeps
two people
together

-commitment

always remember
not to judge people
based on appearances

-appearances

love people
despite their flaws
the most beautiful
shade of love
is
selflessness

-selfess

find someone you want to spend
your sunday mornings with

someone who you want to be around
when things aren't always exciting

find someone whose presence
makes you feel whole
and whose company
makes you full of joy

find someone
you can be
truly
h a p p y
with

-happy

be with someone
who makes the rainy days
feel full of sunlight

-s u n l i g h t

you make the distance
fade away
and i swear i can hear
your laughter
from so many miles away

-miles away

find someone
who loves the parts of you
everyone else
takes for granted

-*soulmate*

you make my mind
l u s t
for you
as much as my body does
and that's
how i know
you're the one

-your lips taste like magic

i watched you become
more and more
in love with yourself
and that
is the most beautiful thing
i have ever seen

-self-love

i wonder, if i told you
the fantasies i've had of you
would you want
to make them real?

-the risk

my darling,
tell me you love me
it's
m u s i c
to my ears

-music

love
is never a question

if you have to ask
"am i in love?"
you aren't.

wait for someone
who makes you feel
so in love
that by comparison
everyone before them
felt like nothing.

-love is never a question

adventure with me
to the mountains
let's find ourselves
in exotic places
and meditate
on our existence

-mountains

Chapter Three

Rising

there is no challenge
so great
that the fire
from deep within your soul
cannot overcome it

-you are more powerful than you know

every loss
is a lesson

every heartbreak
brings you closer to true love

every mistake
brings you closer to truth

nothing is what it seems.

the darkness you are going through
will end
and you will come out of that tunnel
in a more beautiful place
and closer to happiness
than you were before.

-every loss is a lesson

i could look
into your eyes
forever

-eyes

hello, dear one

it has been so long
since we last spoke
that my soul
had begun to forget
the way it felt
to be near you

but one taste
and instantly i'm hooked again

-addict pt. ii

life
is too damn short
to be with someone
who doesn't make you
h a p p y

-life is too short

the first leaves of fall
begin to drift
down from the trees

-autumn beings, oh how beautiful

you might feel broken now
but fear not
the pain will pass
and you will be healed in time.

-time

time passes
all to quickly
with you

-how you know you're in love

social change
will never happen
until each and every one of us
stand up for what's right
in our daily lives

-conviction

men in power
somehow always say
that the fight
for women's equality
is unnecessary
when our president
is a sexual assaulter.

-*dichotomy*

women
are not objects

women
are not toys

women
are not
less than men

-teach your sons

you make me feel
as if
i'm drifting through life
on a cloud

-i feel at peace with you

even the slaughter of children
was not enough
to convince america
to stop clinging
to weapons of murder.

-sometimes it seems like we will never change

no person
in the wealthiest country in history
should go bankrupt
because of a medical issue

if we can afford
a military budget
ten times larger
than our enemies combined
perhaps we can afford
to take care
of our own goddamn people.

-fed up with a broken system

they want to give men free viagra
yet take away women's birth control
and somehow
they don't see
anything wrong with this?

- *"healthcare"*

how many more trees
do we have to chop down
before we realize
that breathable air
is more valuable
than money?

-idiocy of deforestation

i want to live in a world
where women's bodies
aren't held
to impossible standards.

-we shouldn't be told to starve ourselves

it says something about humanity
that we are willing
to let people suffer
in far away places
as long as our commercial items
are a tiny bit cheaper

-do we have no compassion?

love is love.

gay, straight, bi
or anything at all

it's all love
and should be celebrated
as such

-love is love

i try
to drown my feelings for you
in a bottle

-but it never works

Chapter Four

Daydreaming

i look up at the stars
thinking
of life
on other planets
and the different truths
of different places

-daydreaming

be proud
of the person
you
have become

-*proud*

i want to
live life
as more
than
a shadow

-shadow

with your back
against the wall
do the impossible

break out
and take
the day

this
is how
heroes
are made

-how heroes are made

don't listen to anyone
who tells you
you are
hard to love

-that is never true

you
make me feel
like the most
special person
in the entire
universe

-find someone who makes you feel special

there is no use
in being
in a relationship
with someone
if your intentions
aren't
to love them
the way
they deserve
to be loved

-intentions

you are not broken
when your heart
breaks

you are broken
when you let
that stop you
from loving

-*always try again*

we are one
with the mountains
the trees

-gaia

we are all
just captives
of a crazy world
thrown into
all this mess
with no instructions
and no truths
to follow

we are all
just trying
to figure
it all out
together

-figuring it out

in a world of apathy
be the person
who truly cares
and tries to change things
for the better

-the brave ones

never apologize
for feeling deeply

never apologize
for crying
during sad movies

because there is nothing
more beautiful
or pure

than to feel
deeply
and honestly

-beauty of honesty

you
are so much more
than what
you're going
through

-*more*

you
can never
un-love
what you
once loved

and that
is okay

-it's part of who you are

the people
you surround yourself with
can either
build you up
or tear you down

-choose your friends wisely

people want you
to be as miserable
as they are

so don't take
their insults
to heart

they only want
to bring you down
to their level

-when they go low, we go high

make up sex
is an art form

-make me fall in love again

some mysteries
are not meant
to be solved

-and perhaps it's better that way

Chapter Five

Healing

it's never too late
to turn your life around
and create the future
you've always wanted

-potential

love
is the band-aid
that soothes all wounds

-don't hold back

somehow
the better things get
the more miserable
people become

perhaps it's because
of what's inside of us
and not
the world around us

-happiness is not a list of possessions

take me
to the rings of saturn
let's dance
on the clouds of jupiter
and have pluto
all to ourselves

-celestial bodies

life is too short
to be mean to people
or tolerate people
who are mean to you

-kindness makes the world a better place

tell me,
would you throw a lasso
up to the moon
and pull it
back down
for me?

-give me the moon

your value
is not determined
by how much money you have
or a list of possessions

-broken values

life is not something
that is set in stone

life is a fleeting thing
a whisper in a breeze

we have it
for only a moment

-so make every moment count

we don't choose
the cards we're dealt
we only choose
what to do with them

-and that's the most important part

love someone
who makes you feel
the way coffee does

-my love, my caffeine rush

stop making heroes
out of terrible people

-fuck hollywood

if i could
smoke you away
i would

-smoke

it's better
to be
compelling
than likable

-captivate

your promises
about the big things
don't mean anything
if you don't keep
your smallest promises

-promises

don't listen to the nay-sayers.
follow your dreams
even if you aren't
the best
at what you do—
it's better to just do it
and get better at it
rather than throw it all away
just because you weren't
born a genius
in a particular field.

-no one is born a genius

your words
are the sunlight
and i,
a rose
in a windowsill
growing
under the rays
of your kindness

-soleil

healing
is the process
of opening up your wounds
with a surgical precision
and taking out the bullet
before it kills you

-it hurts but it helps

the tree of knowledge
is the temptation
of knowing things
that can only hurt

-ignorance really is bliss

learning to trust again
after someone
has broken it before
is one of the hardest things
to do

-learning to trust again

let go
of your baggage
and fly high

-freedom

thank you for reading my debut poetry book. i don't know if anyone will ever read this, in truth, but i hope that someone does and that it helps them heal.

if by some chance someone really did read this book, please help me get more readers by leaving an amazon review and posting on social media. as a self-published author, i don't have some huge corporation to get this book out— i just have you, if you're really out there. perhaps it's wishful thinking.

if you're reading this, please know that i appreciate you and thank you for letting my words into your life.

—malia k. auri

CPSIA information can be obtained
at www.ICGtesting.com
Printed in the USA
LVOW12s0230081217
559089LV00005B/447/P